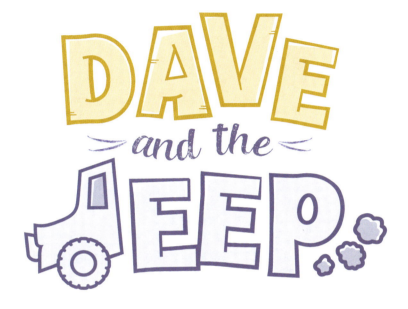

DAVE and the JEEP

Written by

Gracie Phillips

Illustrated by

Ekaterina Kolesnikova

CHAPTER 1

Dave gets up. It is a crisp fall day. Dave feels the breeze.

"Gran is here," Dad says.
"She lost her cat."

"Let us go in the jeep and look for the cat."

Gran packs some things in the jeep.

They get in and go!

The jeep
goes up and
up the hill.
The jeep is at
the top.

Look! Mom's hat. She left it on the hill.

The jeep goes into the mud! *Splash!*

"Oh!" Dave says. "What a mess!"

Look! It is Dave's dog, Pat.
Dave's dog has pups!

They go in the jeep, but still no cat.

Next, they go to the
pond. "Oh!" Dad says. "It is
my sheep."

Dad can lift the black
sheep into the jeep.

Look! It is Ann. "I lost my goat. Can I come?" she says.

"Yes!" Dad says. She sits next to Dave.

Look in the log! Is it
Gran's cat?

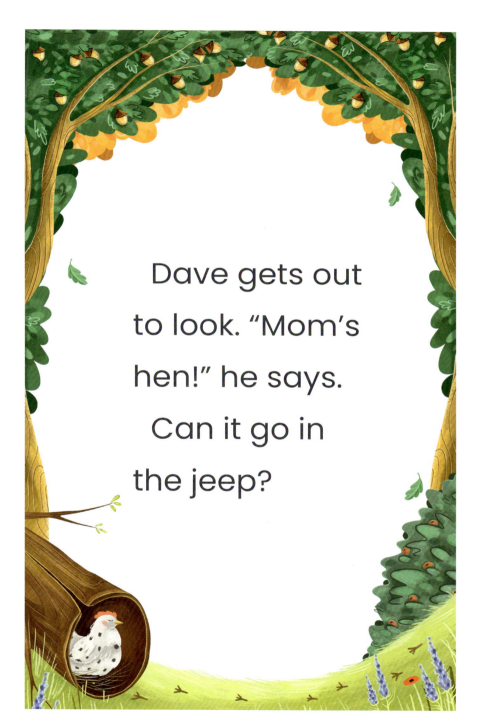

Dave gets out
to look. "Mom's
hen!" he says.
Can it go in
the jeep?

It is so packed! The hen
sits on Dave's lap. *Cluck!*
the hen says.

Still no cat! Dave hugs
Gran. "We can get her," he
says.

CHAPTER 2

The jeep drives into the trees. "Look how red the trees are," Gran says.

"Look at the blue, blue sky," Ann says. Dave loves fall.

"Let's bring some things to Mom," Dave says.

Dad picks these.

Gran gets that one.

Ann gets this.

And Dave gets this one.

"Oh!" Dave says. "Look at the blue thing in that tree. I lost that last spring."

Dad gets up in the tree
to get the kite. They put it
in the jeep.

CHAPTER 3

The jeep goes down the path. A tree is in the way!

Ooooohhhhh no!

Dad and Gran get out of the jeep. Dave and Ann get out of the jeep.

"Three, two, one, push!" says Dad.

They stop to eat some lunch.

Ann and Dave go to the creek. They spy a deer. They spy a pail.

"That is my pail," Dave yells. "I left it here the last time we came."

Dave puts the pail in the jeep.

The jeep starts to go. It is so snug, but Dave loves to feel the breeze.

"Let us go off the path," Dad says. "The cat could be in the tall grass."

"Wait!" Ann calls. "I hear a bell."

"I hear it too," says Dad.

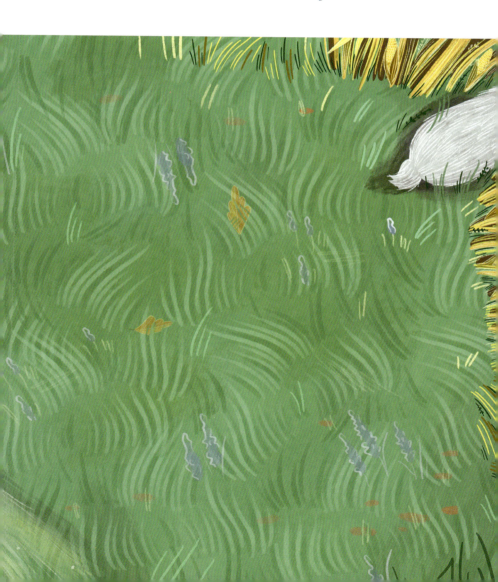

"It is the bell of my goat," says Ann. "The sound is in the corn."

"It is your goat," Gran says. "We found your goat but not my cat."

"We should turn back
and go home," Dad says.
"We are far, and it will take
a long time."

"Let us play a game as we drive," says Ann. "Let's spy as many kinds of birds as we can."

The game is a lot of fun.

Dave sees
these birds.

Ann sees this one.

Gran sees these two.

Dad sees
a big one!

And Dad sees a little one.

Dave sees
two more.
He wins!

The sun starts to set as the jeep bumps home.

Gran is sad. Her cat was not found.

Look! Look by the door. It is Gran's cat!

"Yay!" says Dave.

"Yay," say Gran and Dad and Ann. "We found the cat!"

Mom steps out.

"Yes, Gran's cat came right after you left!"

They all sit in front of the
fire, and Gran holds the
cat on her lap.

Dad and Dave sit by the fire. Well . . . they sleep by the fire.